PwP Publishing
P. O. Box 565
Trenton, NC 28585

Books by the Author

Seven C's of Success—Developing the Attributes, Attitudes and Behaviors to Achieve All You Want Out of Life (2013)

Defining Your Success—You Decide What You Want Out of Life (2013)

When Justice Calls—A novel (2013)

Of Life, Love and Learning—Selected Poems and Educational Raps, Rhythms and Rhymes (2012)

English Grammar and Writing Made Easy—Learn to Communicate More Accurately, Clearly and Concisely (2012)

Personal Care Journal-The Adult Years (2000, co-authored)

A Little Book of Big Principles-Values and Virtues for a More Successful Life (1998 and 2012)

Traffic Signs on the Road of Life (2012), co-authored with Cynthia Brower

Me Teacher, Me...Please!— Observation about Parents, Students, Teachers and the Teaching-Learning Process (2001)

Visit the Author's Amazon Page:

http://tinyurl.com/ckw5ms8

WHAT A DIFFERENCE A COMMA MAKES—

The Complete Guide for Understanding

and

Applying Correctly Punctuation Marks

and

Symbols Commonly Used In English Grammar

WHAT A DIFFERENCE A COMMA MAKES

Copyright © 2015 by Wilbur L. Brower, Ph.D.

Library of Congress Control Number: 2015956958

Brower, Wilbur L.

1. Punctuations   2. Grammar

3. Writing

Correspondence to the author should be directed to:

PwP Publishing
P. O. Box 565
Trenton, NC 28585

E-mail: wlbrower@gmail.com

ISBN: 978-0-9894838-5-8

DEDICATION

This small effort is dedicated to all the students at

Jacksonville Commons Middle School

Jacksonville, North Carolina,

who can change the world by unleashing the

Power of their Potential.

Table of Contents

Preface

The idea for this publication began several years ago after a discussion I had with a student who was struggling to pass ninth-grade English/Language Arts. He was performing very poorly in the class, but he asserted that he did not have to do "my" work because he was an athlete. He was very confident that he was going to be the next high school and college superstar and did not need to know what I was teaching. He was also very confident that he would become a professional athlete.

First, I disabused him of the notion that he was learning anything for "me," but that anything he was learning was for himself. Then I demonstrated to him how I could change one comma in a sentence and change the meaning of the entire paragraph. I think he was intrigued by the notion that I could do that, but he still neglected to study and learn what was required for him to earn a passing grade in the class.

He made no effort to do what was expected of him in the classroom, but he continued to participate in two or three sports. Unfortunately for him, he did not earn a passing grade in the class he took with me.

Ten years later and finding myself back in the classroom after being retired for three years, I've seen a greater need for a publication of this nature now, more than ever before. I've seen a significant decline in the use of conventions of grammar and writing, and I attribute much of it to the increase in texting and the constant use of social media.

What a Difference a Comma Makes is intended to reach young adults like the one mentioned above, as well as anyone struggling to use punctuations correctly, providing them a ready reference that can improve their writing skills or enhance their academic success. I've attempted to demonstrate the importance of conveying the message the writer intended, rather than an unintended message or one that can be misconstrued or misunderstood because of faulty or incorrect punctuations.

While this small publication is not intended to be an exhaustive authority on punctuations, it is a rather compact and comprehensive work that will help resolve most confusions about the most appropriate and effective ways of using them.

INTRODUCTION

Punctuations are simply **sign** or *marks* used in a written sentence to make it easy to read and understand. They are ways of conveying the exact intended meaning of spoken language. Punctuation marks dictate the flow of ideas and thoughts in a sentence. They are similar to a traffic cop who, in order to ensure an orderly flow, controls the traffic as it makes its way either through a busy city street or along a country road. Punctuation marks are used to help the reader decipher accurately the message a written passage contains or intends to convey. In other words, the essential purpose of punctuation marks is to clarify ideas and thoughts. If punctuation marks are used *incorrectly*, the written passage may contain *inaccurate* or *unintended* messages.

Different punctuation marks serve different purposes. Some separate ideas and words; others place emphasis on ideas and words; yet, others categorize and group together related ideas and words, or ensure that they remain together. Without clear punctuation marks, written materials would be confusing, misleading or misunderstood.

Rules for punctuation are easy to understand and apply, but first they must be learned and used in ways they are intended, not in ways the writer chooses to use them or is accustomed to using them. This section will explain how to use the more common punctuations that writers are likely to encounter in everyday usage.

Signs or **Symbols** represent or stand for something else, especially material objects representing something abstract. *There* are images that are often used to support text, making the meaning clearer and easier to understand.

The publication is divided into three distinct sections: *End Marks*, *Grammatical Punctuations* and *Signs and Symbols*. While I am not sure that there is such "official" categorizations or designations of punctuations and signs and symbols as done here, I have *elected* to do it, nevertheless. This, I believe, makes more practical sense than it probably does in a conventional or linguistic sense. Each section contains a brief explanation and descriptions of its contents.

PART I
End Marks

. ? !

The End Marks are the period, the question mark, and the exclamation point or mark.

They are used at the end of a sentence to control the flow and tempo. All three end

marks are punctuations that serve the same function: to indicate that the sentence is to

get a full stop. To use driving analogies, the period, the question mark and the

exclamation point are equivalent to a red light or stop sign.

●

The Period (.) is used at the end of every sentence except a **direct** question or an exclamation.

> Examples: We will have the quiz next Friday.
>
> The report looks just fine. I thinks it's good to go.
>
> I asked where I could buy oranges for a good price. (This is an **indirect** question.)
>
> The direct question would be: Where can I buy oranges for a good price?

After a Non-sentence

> Examples: Good Afternoon.
>
> Good Morning.

The period indicates that the message or thought is complete and does not need any other punctuations to convey its meaning. The period means there is a complete break.

Do **not** add a period if the last item in the sentence is an abbreviation that ends in a period.

> Examples; The letter should go to Gail Pylant, Ed. D.
>
> Please eat, brush your teeth, shower, etc.

?

The Question Mark (?) is used: After a Direct Question

Examples: Where are you going?

What time is it?

In statements ending with a word inflected as a question and with question tags.

Examples: Just leave these papers on Marco's desk, OK?

So you made the JCMS Principal's List, eh?

To turn a statement into a question, which gives the impression that the speaker is assuming or hoping for a certain reply.

Examples: You promise to finish going through those records?Isabell didn't actually hit him?

After a direct question, which is inserted into a statement. If the question comes at the end, separate it with a comma. Capitalization of the question after the comma is used for extreme emphasis but is rarely recommended.

Examples: His boss wondered, Was he really doing his job the best he could?

Within Parentheses to Indicate Doubt or Uncertainty

Examples: The school opened in 1954 (?) and closed in 2004.

The feature movie starts at 8:15 p. m. (?)

If the inserted question comes in the beginning of the sentence, put the question mark in the middle, but do not capitalize the word following it.

Example: Was she really doing her job the best she could? her boss wondered.

Was Mariella really doing the best she could? was the question.

The question is, is Ada really doing the best she can?

You didn't find those documents, did you? [Question tag]

You found those documents, didn't you? [Question tag]

You're not leaving right now, are you?

!

The Exclamation Point (!), also referred to as an exclamation mark, is used to express or emphasize strong feelings. The punctuation was originally referred to as the "note of admiration." Exclamations can be a single word, several words, a complete sentence, or introductory word to a sentence that conveys astonishment or surprise.

Single Word

Examples: Fantastic!

Wow!

Several Words

Examples: What a shot!

Way to go!

Holy Mackerel!

Complete Sentence

Example: I can't believe she got that scholarship!

I am really excited!

Introductory Word to a Sentence

Examples: Oh! That's right. I forgot.

No! That's all wrong.

Typically, only one exclamation point is used. In informal writing, however, many

people use multiple exclamation points to express the degree of their excitement.

Examples: What do you mean you forgot my iPhone!!!!!

No!!!! Jared has already told you a thousand times!

PART II
GRAMMATICAL
PUNCTUATIONS

, ; : ' " " – ... ***

End Marks control what happens at the end of a sentence; they are the stop signs at the end of the road. The Grammatical Punctuations, on the other hand, are other road signs placed along the internal sentence highway of our writing to control speed, provide directions, prevent head-on collisions of ideas and convey the intended message. When placed in the correct place of a sentence, grammatical punctuations define parameters of thoughts, increase clarity, and eliminate or reduce confusion.

Grammatical Punctuations are essential for establishing context and giving sentence structures their intended meanings. Without Grammatical Punctuations, written words can take on a variety of different meaning, determined almost exclusively by the reader. Grammatical Punctuations, in essence, are the road map between the beginning and ending of a sentence, and they provide the details, the contours and the nuances of the journey.

,

The Comma (,) is a flashing yellow light that asks the driver to slow down and proceed with caution. It is used to note a break in the flow of a sentence, and it is the most misused of all punctuation marks and accounts for more than half of all punctuation errors. Therefore, more space will be dedicated to this punctuation challenge than to the others. In fact, there are more than twenty rules, depending on how you're counting, for using commas correctly. These rules demonstrate how to punctuate more clearly and effectively to ensure that accurate and intended passages are contained in written materials.

Use the comma to set off:

1. **Independent or main clauses**—A comma follows the first of **two independent clauses** that are joined by coordinating conjunctions (*for, and, nor, but, or, yet,* and *so*):

   Examples: The story's main character is Sasha, **and** its author is Sy Oliver.

   Oliver's early stories were more popular, **but** his later ones have failed.

Note that the comma comes **before** the conjunction.

Do not use a comma if there is not a full clause after the conjunction.

   Wrong: Sasha barked loudly, and jumped on her bed.

Right: Sasha barked loudly and jumped on her bed.

Sasha is the subject of *barked loudly* and *jumped on the bed.*

2. **Items in a series**—Use commas to separate clauses, phrases and words in a series of three or more. The comma is often referred to as the serial or Oxford comma, and it precedes the conjunction before the final item in the list of items.

Examples: **Clauses:** Carol took Spanish classes, she studied cooking, and she worked a part-time job.

Phrases: The video is available in the JCMS media center, in some classrooms, and at several video rental shops in Jacksonville.

Words: I enjoy the writings of Steinbeck, Cooper, Grisham, and Hemingway.

3. **Introductory Devices**—Use commas to introduce:

Introductory Word: Use commas only after introductory words that receive special emphasis.

Examples: **Conversely**, you could listen. Then Joshua can go home.

Understandably, Emma was upset about what happened.

Yes, the books should be delivered to Ms. Brannon early tomorrow morning.

However, you will be satisfied with the results.

Common introductory words like *however, furthermore, meanwhile* and

still are used to create continuity from one sentence to the next.

An introductory adverb clause:

Example: **If you pay my cell phone bill today**, I'll repay you tomorrow.

Introductory clauses begin with adverbs such as *after, although, as, because, before, if, since, though, until* and *when.*

A long prepositional phrase at the beginning of a sentence:

Examples: **In the middle of a hot summer day**, we went for a long walk along the beach.

On his way to Bermuda, Tyrese made a detour to the Bahamas.

Do not use a comma if the long prepositional phrase is at the end of the sentence.

Examples: We went for a walk along the beach in the middle of the day.

Tyrese made a detour to the Bahamas on his way to Bahamas.

4. **Parenthetical Phrases**—or expressions are words or groups of **words that** interrupt the main flow, idea or thought of a sentence. While parenthetical expressions are not essential to the meaning of the sentence, they provide additional information about it. There are several types of parenthetical expressions.

Examples: This book report, **in my opinion**, is one of the best.

That book report, **on the other hand,** is not too bad.

5. **A Nonrestrictive or Nonessential Clause** is parenthetical. This clause gives information that is not essential to the meaning of the sentence. Therefore, you may omit or take out the clause and still get the meaning of the sentence. The parenthetical clause is set off with comma.

Examples: Commons Drive, **which runs alongside the school**, is always busy.

Commons Drive is always busy.

Coach Foust, **who attended Ohio State University**, won the first State Championship for the school.

Coach Foust won the first State Championship for the school.

A restrictive clause is important to the meaning of the sentence. It gives additional information about a preceding noun in the sentence and answers the question "which one?" Restrictive clauses are not set off by commas.

Examples: The car **that she bought** was recalled.

The man **who lives next door** is an Air Force veteran.

Without these clauses, the sentences could refer to any car or any man.

6. **A Nonrestrictive or Nonessential Phrase—This phrase gives** information that is not essential to the meaning of the sentence. Therefore, you may omit or take out the phrase and still get the meaning of the sentence. The parenthetical phrase is set off with comma.

Examples: Cynthia, **wearing a red scarf**, is Sheila's best friend.

The S-500 Mercedes, **with the red bow**, is her birthday present.

7. **Coordinate Adjectives**—In a series of two or more, use commas to separate adjectives of equal value or importance. Do not use a comma after the last adjective in the series.

Examples: The **tall**, **statuesque** woman over there is a model.

Crude, profane or vulgar language is not tolerated here.

8. **Names and Other Words Used in Direct Address:**

Examples: **Zyiiah**, when are you going to Atlanta?

For my senior project, **Mr. Curry**, I'm producing a DVD.

9. **Yes or No at the Beginning of a Sentence:**

Examples: **No**, I don't expect to attend the ceremony.

Yes, I am leaving for Wilmington early tomorrow morning.

10. **Direct Quotations**—Use commas to separate a direct quote from the preceding or following words.

Examples: "I'm not going to take it anymore," Gizelle said.

"Of all days," Gabe said, "you had to come home today without your iPod."

11. **Before a Confirmatory Question, or to separate a statement from a question:**

Examples: It's about time to go, isn't it?

You're not leaving now, **are you?**

12. **Comma and Abbreviations:** These abbreviations: Sr. (*senior*), Jr. (*junior*), and etc. (*et cetera*) are always preceded by a comma. Don't place commas after these abbreviations.

Examples: Howard, Sr. had Howard, Jr. to get the mail, water the horses, cut grass, etc.

Kareem Williams, Jr. is a superb wrestler.

13. **Set off Geography Names:** Place commas between related geographical place names and after the last place name, unless it appears at the end of a sentence.

Examples: Ronald lived in Charlotte, NC, for a year.

Jacquill has always wanted to live in San Francisco, CA.

When the place name is a possessive, this rule does not apply

Examples: Charlotte, NC's traffic is almost always congested.

Wilmington, NC's major university is UNC-W.

14. **Set off Professional Titles:** Place a comma after abbreviated professional titles if they occur in the middle of a sentence.

Examples: Dominique Jackson, Ph. D., will be the guest speaker for the next annual conference.

Deoviona Worley, M.D., and Angie Perdom, D. D. S., are best friends.

15. **Dates:** Use commas to separate number dates and years. Because different style

    manuals offer different opinions about this usage, you may or may not place a

    comma following the year.

    Examples: March 11, 1999, was the day we went there.

    On March 12, 1999 we went back home.

16. **Commas to Enclose Parenthetical Expressions:** Use commas before and after

    words that interrupt the flow of the sentence. If the interruption is minimal, you may leave out the commas.

    Examples: The best way to see the game, **if you can afford it**, is in person.

    The timing **for me** could not have been worse.

17. **Comma and Duplicate Words:** Place commas between repeated words when needed to improve clarity.

    Examples: Alexia and Brighton moved **in, in** May.

    The utilities were turned **on, on** May first.

    This confusion can be eliminated by re-writing the sentence.

    Examples: It was in May that Alexia and Brighton moved in.

    May first is when the utilities were turned on

18. **Comma to Replace Missing Words: Use commas to replace omitted** words, especially the word *that*.

    Examples: Andru is a vegetarian; his wife, a meat-eater.

    Win some, lose some.

    What I mean is, Kylee hasn't changed her diet and followed mine.

19. **Comma to Separate Comparisons or to Indicate a Deliberate Pause or Shift**

Examples: Dylan is simply tired, not lazy.

Javion is very intelligent, even brilliant.

20. **Comma in Parenthetical Citations:** Place a comma after each author's name,

except the last in a multiple author citation. **Don't** use a comma between the author(s) and the page number(s) and dates.

Examples: (Ellis, Geffre, Ly and Smith 14)

(Hall, Quickley, Cobb and McGhee 2015)

Don't place a comma between different authors or resource titles citing information; use a semicolon.

Examples: (Allen, Laws and Lonegran 28; Martin, Napier, McVarish 2014)

(Harris, Mc Intyre and Fanning 2015; Nino, Sanders and Sullivan 126)

21. **Appositive:** Use commas to set apart appositives. An appositive is a noun or pronoun placed next to another noun or pronoun to identify, define, or describe it. The appositive can be a word, phrase, or clause.

Examples: That man, the one with the hat, left town quickly.

Ms. Holly, our school receptionist, has a very pleasing voice and bubbly personality.

22. **Compound Sentence:** Use commas before coordinating conjunctions to join two independent clauses if one or more of the sentences is long.

Examples: Aldrion liked her, *and* she definitely said that she liked him.

This always annoyed Ada, and she made sure everybody felt her wrath when she was upset.

23. Speaker Tag: In dialogue sentences, place commas before and after a middle speaker tag to the left of both quotation marks. Question marks and exclamation points can also separate speaker tags from dialogue.

Examples: "But if you don't press," Shyheim shouted, "you will never win."

"That was a well-developed paper," Brendan said, "but I think mine is much better."

;

The Semicolon (;) is a stop sign that tells us to ease gradually to a halt, before gradually starting up again. It is a period above a comma and indicates that there is a greater break in a thought than the comma but a lesser break than the period. The semicolon is often interchangeable with the period.

Us the semicolon:

Between Independent Clauses Not Joined by a Coordinating Conjunction.

Semicolons are often used to replace a period if the writer *intends* to narrow the space between two closely linked sentences.

Examples: World War I was rough; World War II was rougher.

Call Mrs. Washington at school; she should be there by now.

Call Angel tomorrow; you can give her your answer then.

Shilo paid his fees; he expects access to all amenities the club offers.

Between Independent Clauses Joined by a Conjunctive Adverb (*also, besides consequently; furthermore, however, in fact; likewise, meanwhile, nevertheless; otherwise, still, therefore; then* and *thus*).

Examples: The store was closed; however, Zhyshawn, the manager, let us in.

It's getting late; therefore, Radell must leave now.

Between Items in a Series When There Are Commas within the Items—Add a semicolon after every three items in the series.

Examples: We had chicken, rice, string beans; corn, potato salad; biscuits, cornbread, banana pudding; chocolate cake, ice-cream and iced-tea.

All we need are paper, pencils, flash drives; directions, sign-in sheets and locations.

The Colon (:) is used to introduce:

A List of Something or Things That Follow:

Examples: Saunti received the award for one reason: her scholarship.

The first team consists of four sophomores: Tre'Quan, Jaylon, Cole and Caden.

Do not use a colon before a list when it directly follows a **verb** or **preposition**.

Examples: Alex wants: apples, bananas and oranges. (**Incorrect** because it follows the verb **want.**)

Alex wants the following: apples, bananas and oranges. (**Correct**)

A colon may be used between independent clauses when the second sentence expands, paraphrases, explains or builds on the first sentence.

Examples: Nathaniel got what he worked for: he studied hard for those grades.

All is well with Christopher now: his dog has returned.

Syncere has one goal: to win the top math prize

Use a colon to follow the salutation in a business letter, even if you are addressing a person by his or her first name,

Examples: Dear Mrs. Hendricks:

Dear Colby:

A Long Quotation (usually one or more paragraphs):

When quotations are introduced by a colon, it is unnecessary to surround them with quotations marks.

Example: In the beginning of novel <u>Uncle Tom's Cabin</u>, Harriet Beecher Stowe wrote:

Late in the afternoon on a chilly day in February, two gentlemen were sitting alone over their wine, in a well-furnished dining parlor, in the town of P___, in Kentucky. There were no servants present, and the gentlemen, with chairs closely approaching, seemed to be discussing some subject with great earnestness.

Use a quotation mark at the end of a long quote **if the last sentence contains a quote**.

Example: In the classic novel <u>The Outsiders</u>, author S. E. Hinton wrote:

In some small town in the late 1950's there are two gangs of teenage boys: One is the Greasers. They are the working class, "poor" boys. The other is the Soc. They are the upper class, "rich" kids. The Soc describe Greasers as, "White trash with long, greasy hair." While the Greasers describe the Soc as, "White trash with mustangs and madras."

,

The Apostrophe (') is used to:

Form the Possessive Case of Singular and Plural Nouns

Examples: This is the boy's coat.

These are the boys' coats.

The woman's dress is here.

The women's dresses are here.

Show Contractions and Other Omission of Letters or Numerals

Examples: don't (do not)

who's (who is)

class of '85 (1985)

For the Plurals of Letters, Numbers, Symbols and Words

Examples: Gabrielle made all A's.

Xavier uses too many and's in his writings.

Dalvin's career peaked in the 1990's.

" "

Quotation Marks are a pair of punctuation marks typically used to mark the beginning and end of a passage attributed to someone and repeated word-for-word.

Examples: Adriel said, "I'm certain that we're going to Atlanta this summer."

"You'll be sorry about this," Keyshawn stated emphatically.

Quotation marks are also used to convey the sense of something that is unusual or in doubt.

Examples: Thank you for "helping" me.

Brandon has a "tough guy" reputation.

Single quotation marks are used inside of double quotation marks to identify a quote within a quote.

Examples: Chase told me, "Alyssa said, 'I'm tired of keying all those letters.'" The *Jacksonville Daily News* Sports Reporter told me, "When I interviewed JCMS star player Marquez Hayward, he said they simply 'played a better game.'"

Notice that what Alyssa and Marquez said was enclosed in single quotation marks. Also notice that the period was placed inside both the single and the double quotation marks.

How to handle a quote within a quote within a quote:

Example: "Makayla said, 'Ashley, if you say "hell" again, I'm going to tell your Mom.' "

Note that the word "hell" is in double quotes.

The Hyphen (-) is used to:

Join Certain Compound Words:

Examples: brother-in-law

Hop-scotch

Attorneys-at-Law

Sergeant-at-Arms

Join Words Used as a Single Adjective before a Noun:

Examples: Western Boulevard is a **well-traveled** street.

Wyatt is a **much-admired** student.

Colby was a so-so basketball player, but a great trainer.

Write Two-Word Numbers from 21-99 and Two-Word Fractions:

Examples: twenty-five   two-thirds

sixty-first   three-fourths

Introduce the Prefixes *ex* and *self*, and the suffix *elect*:

Examples: Bill Clinton is an ex-president.

Nivia has a lot of self-confidence.

President-elect Obama was sworn in on January 20, 2009.

Divide a Word That Will Not Fit at the End of a Sentence:

Examples: The classroom is too small to **accom-**
modate all the students.

That requires us to have a **tempo-**
rary staging area.

The hyphen has to be placed between two syllables.

✳ ✳ ✳

● ● ●

Ellipses Marks are usually represented by three periods, but three asterisks are occasionally used. (An ellipsis is the singular form of ellipses, meaning only mark, but they are always used in pairs.) They are also referred to as "*dot-dot-dot.*" Ellipses marks are used in writing or printing to show an omission, especially omissions and **leaving out** letters or words.

Examples: "After school Caleb went to her house, which was a few blocks away, and then went home."

"After school Caleb went to her house ... and then went home."

Ellipses are often used to show a **pause** in a thought or to create **suspenseful** feelings in the reader. (*Suspense* is when a reader starts feeling anxious to know what is going to happen next.)

Examples: Jazlyn opened the door . . . and saw . . . a huge box!

Kailey was thinking . . . maybe they should call home.

Ellipses are used to show a break, or trailing off, of a thought or idea.

Examples: I can't imagine...

"I'm not sure what to do . . .," Porsha said.

PART III
BRACKETS

( )   [ ]   { }   < >

Brackets are pairs of devices used to insert words that are further explanations or are

considered as a group. They are used in writing for showing that some information

within the sentence can be considered separately. Brackets are also used in mathematics

for showing that a set of numbers between them can be considered separately.

( )

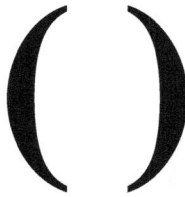

Parentheses [( )], also known as *round* or *curved brackets*, are used to:

Set off incidental information:

Examples: Senator Elizabeth Dole (R., NC) will leave the U. S. Congress in January 2009.

Enclose references, numbers and questions marks:

Examples: The picture (see page 125) is very beautiful.

Jasmine has authority to (1) tutor, (2) impose discipline, and (3) check notebooks.

The school opened in 1954 (?) and closed in 2004.

Mark off a parenthetical word or phrase:

Examples: (See Figure 3 below.)

Ms. Queen verified Lamar's high school diploma (Northside High School, class of 2015), but his work history remains unconfirmed.

Regardless of the information the writer chooses to include in parentheses, it must not be a grammatically integral part of the remainder of the sentence.

Time zones are usually enclosed in parentheses following the time:

Example: The FBLA Annual Conference will begin at 9:00 a.m. (EST).

[ ]

These brackets, also known as square brackets, are used primarily in technical explanations. In academic writing, brackets are used to enclose the Latin word sic, which means "so, thus." The [sic] is used to denote an error that originally appears in the source material and is not attributable to the author who is using the quote.

Examples: The final report stated that "all of them was [sic] responsible for the accident."

Xzarviera wrote, "She made there [sic] beds before they came back home."

If you use italics to emphasize a portion of a quotation, the change in the quote must be noted in the brackets.

Example: Alice said she would consider "a very short extension of the deadline, but only under *extraordinary circumstances* [emphasis added]."

One common place to find brackets is in dictionaries.

{   }

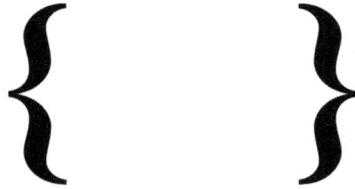

Braces, or curly brackets, are marks that have extremely limited usage. They are typically used to contain two or more lines of text or listed items to show that they are a group. Braces are quite common in mathematics and science, and they are often used in music and poetry. An exception to this would be if a writer wanted to create a list of items that are all equal choices.

Examples: Equal choices: Choose a color {blue, red, white, pink} to paint the room.

Music chords: [{c, e, g} {e, g, c2} {g, c2, e2}]

Number set: {2, 4, 6, 8, 10, 12}

Otherwise, this punctuation mark would not be used in academic or literary writing.

< >

Angled brackets have very limited use in writing, but they are used in various computer programming languages. During the early days of the Internet, they were used primarily for placing URL's (Universal Resource Locator) or an email address into text.

Examples: Dr. Brower's information is at
<www.wlbrower.com>.

He also can be reached at <wlbrower@gmail.com>.

It was thought that the inclusion of angled brackets would eliminate any confusion that might result from certain punctuation marks and words surrounding URL's or email addresses.

Some style manuals no longer require URLs to be presented because of their ever changing status. However, some professors and teachers may still require students to include the URL. If the URL is required, the web address needs to be placed between a pair of angled brackets.

Angled brackets should not be used to replace parentheses or braces.

Part IV

SIGNS & SYMBOLS

& @ *

While signs and symbols are often considered synonymous, they have quite different definitions, and they serve very different functions in writing. A symbol is something that represents something else through association or resemblance. A symbol is a sign, emblem or an image. In writing, letters or characters are symbols. A sign, by contrast, can be described as an indicator, a clue, hint, reminder, gesture or a cue. A sign used by a brand is known as a trademark. Signs refer to objects in a more literal way, such as depicting, pointing something out or standing for something.

# #

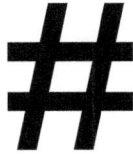

Number/Pound/Hashtag—traditionally, the # symbol has been called the **pound sign** and the **number sign.** It was called a pound sign because the symbol comes from the abbreviation for weight, lb, or "libra pondo," which literally means "a pound by weight." Now, the symbol is also called a **hashtag,** and it is being used for **"hashtagging"** on social media websites.

Examples: Marseille is Baine's #1 fan.

#1 Cincinnati Royals

#jcmscte/facebook

#letsdoitjcms/instagram

The # symbol is also used as a proofreader's mark to indicate the need to insert a space

between lines of text or space between words:

#

Examples: Alia needs moretime to finish her project.

If I had known you were coming. #

I would have baked a cake or two.

&

The **ampersand** (&) is a symbol for the word "and." The ampersand is not typically used in general writing or text to abbreviate the word *and*.

Example: Dezmond needs to go to the Media Center immediately **&** talk with Ms. Mundy. (Incorrect)

Dezmond needs to go to the Media Center immediately **and** talk with Ms. Mundy. (Correct)

It is permissible to use the ampersand in official names of companies.

Examples: Luna, Martinez & Johnson Athletic Consulting and Training Services

Proctor & Gamble

Smith & Wesson

The ampersand may be used in a table where there is a lot of text and space is very limited.

AVAILABLE	DESCRIPTION	NEIGHBORHOOD
11 Nov 2015	5-Bd. Rm, off-street parking, & large backyard	Broadell/E. E. Smith
1 Dec 2015	Tommy Bahama Collection & Other high-ends	No. Raleigh, NC

At least until well into the nineteenth century, the ampersand was treated as the twenty-seventh letter of the alphabet.

The *at* Sign or Symbol stands for many different things, depending upon the country and language of use, and there is no officially-recognized or universal name for it. However, it is universally associated with email addresses.

 Examples: kyeeniahy@gmail.edu

     Uniqued@gmail.com

Before the @ symbol became the standard symbol for e-mail, it was typically used to indicate the cost or weight of something.

 Examples: 5 Gala Apples @ $.75 ea.

     3 Arrey Kono Dresses @ $1,999.95 ea.

The @ symbol is used in several countries around the world to associate its shape with some kind of animal.

 Examples: Apenstaartje—Dutch for "monkey's tail"

     Dalphaengi—Korean for "snail"

     Grisehal—Norwegian for "pig's tail"

     Klammeraffe—German for "hanging monkey"

     Sobachka—Russian for "little dog"

✳

The Asterisk (*) is a symbol used for various reasons in printing and writing, and is most often used to denote an absence or omission of information, or to refer a reader to a notation. The word "asterisk" comes from the Latin word "asteriscus" and the Greek word "asterikos" meaning "little star."

The asterisk is used to:

- indicate a footnote at the bottom of the page.

  Example: All Books 25 % off

  Today Only! *

  _____

  * Discount is good for in-store and online.

- A **footnote** is an explanation or a comment at the bottom of a page that refers back to a specific part of the text.

- If there is more than on footnote, use one asterisk for the first footnote, two asterisks for the second and so on.

  *first footnote

  **second footnote

  ***third footnote

A footnote should begin on the bottom of the same page on which the asterisk symbol appears. Also, in**sure that footnotes at the bottom of the page match the asterisks in the original text.**

- indicate there is an omission of materials in a paper or a report and refers to a body of text that is too large to include. Place an asterisk next to reference point and then at the bottom of the page give a fuller explanation of the source.

    Example: The detailed analysis the JCMS CTE Teachers prepared is in a report* that was disseminated to all staff.

    ---

    * See The Changed and Changing Nature of School and Work (2014), which examines some of the challenges of providing students learning experiences that will prepare them for the real-world of work.

- **edit or substitute letters in profanity or swear words in informal text.**

    Examples: Oh, s****!

    She screamed, "D***!" as her hand slowly lost its grip during the high-wire act.

- **provide emphasis in place of boldface.**

    Examples: You *must* go there — the food is awesome!

    Ginuwine says he really *loves* school.

REFERENCES

https://www.google.com/#safe=strict&q=how+to+use+asterisk+in+writing (Accessed: November 4, 2015)

MLA Style Manual. Walter S. Achtert and Joseph Gibaldi. New York: Modern Language Association, 1985.

Publication Manual of the American Psychological Association, 6th ed. Washington, DC: American Psychological Association, 2010.

R.M. Ritter, ed., *The Oxford Style Manual.* Oxford University Press, 2003.

Tapella, Robert C. *U.S. Government Printing Office Style Manual*, Washington, DC: U. S. Government, 2010.

The Chicago Manual of Style, 16th Edition. Chicago: University of Chicago Press, 2010.

Trimble, John R. *Writing with Style—Conversations on the Art of Writing.* Prentice-Hall, Inc.: Upper Saddle Brook, NJ, 2000.

Turabian, Kate L. A Manual for Writers of Term Papers, Theses, and Dissertations (Chicago Guides to Writing, Editing, and Publishing) 6th Edition. Chicago: University of Chicago Press, 1996

Webster's New World Dictionary. New York: Wiley Publishing, 2003.

White, E. B. and William Strunk, Jr. *The Elements of Style.* Ithaca, NY: Cornell University